Waqas Khwaja has not only published his own poems in *Atlanta Review*, but edited a remarkable Pakistan Issue for the journal in 2014. Deeply steeped in both Eastern and Western cultures, he negotiates the gulf between them as few other writers can. Khwaja's poetry is unfailingly subtle, witty, and intelligent. And his heart is big enough to encompass the joy and suffering, the tragedies and ironies that our increasingly global civilization confronts us with.

Dan Veach (founding editor of *Atlanta Review*, author of *Elephant Water*, editor & translator of *Flowers of Flame*, winner of the Willis Barnstone Translation Prize)

In *Hold Your Breath* Waqas Khwaja catches the fleeting nature of love, life and memories, and doing it he takes us on a sublime journey moving back and forth in space and time. Poetry is sound first and his experiments with sounds and syllables, particularly in his poems 'piya tore nain' and 'Primer', stand out as fresh and innovative.

Abhay K. (winner of the SAARC Literary award for poetry)

The modern world may only be confronted with a heart that is heroic and tender. Waqas Khwaja's *Hold Your Breath* delivers the perfect poems for this collapsing world, contrasting idyllic memory with contemporary clashes of age, gender, and culture. This tale is not for the faint-hearted, but the message is for every one of us.

Youssef Aloui (author of *Fiercer Monsters*)

Waqas Khwaja is a master of his medium. His poems go beyond imagination and incantation. We, his readers, find ourselves inside circles the poet closes just before we catch our breath.

Franklin Abbott (poet, psychotherapist, activist)

A sustained lyricism with a hard but compassionate look at the worlds around him—a desolate but beloved homeland, a new World, love and violence— Waqas Khwaja, with the range of a magpie mastering both memory and modernity, holds our breath in his hands poem after poem as we listen with wonder to a poet who knows words like us are clay birds that must sing even in the darkness of our Time: "You give them your breath /you give them your voice/it's almost as if/they stir in your hands."

Kerry Keys (poet and translator)

Anger, nostalgia, evocative eroticism and amorphous love for the universal characterise his work. In his short and bilingual poems the poetry comes into its element of play with words, rhythms, images, sensuousness and games of hide and seek. He establishes his identity as a person from the Third World but a poet of universal awareness.

Dileep Jhaveri (poet & playwright, winner of the Jayant Pathak Award for poetry)

Waqas Khwaja's *Hold Your Breath* asks the reader to stop, think, and then feel. The language of his poetry has the essence of Sufi thinking, which too asks one to pause, to hold one's breath for deeper awareness. But the poet is not repeating old Sufi ways of thinking. He recreates them in his own way, in his own philosophy in a very different atmosphere. The inner soul of his poetry borrows its thread from Sufism.

Rati Saxena (poet, vedic scholar, and editor of on-line journal *kritya*)

Compassion, concurrence, and creativity are hallmarks of the poetry of Waqas Khwaja, as it ranges, sometimes bilingually, from his native Pakistan to a new home in America and the world that includes not only Emily Dickinson and centaurs dancing, but also Islamophobia and the blinding effects of living in the land of the Cyclopes. We have to hold our breath with Eric Garner, if we wish to breathe.

Yiorgos Chouliaras (Greek poet & essayist, founding editor of *Tram* and *Hartis*)

Khwaja is a committed poet, committed to speaking out against injustice. He may be anywhere, but he will not be silent about injustice, not take refuge merely in his artistic sensibility. For he is not an artist who does not think about his work. Perhaps more than in his previous collections, he has written poems about writing poetry.

M. A. Niazi (Exective Editor, *The Nation*, Lahore)

Waqas Khwaja, professor of English at Agnes Scott College, has published three collections of poetry, *No One Waits for the Train*, *Six Geese from a Tomb at Medum*, and *Mariam's Lament*, in addition to a literary travelogue, *Writers and Landscapes*, recounting his experiences with the International Writers Program, University of Iowa, and several edited anthologies of Pakistani literature in translation. He served as translation editor and contributor for *Modern Poetry of Pakistan*, and has guest edited special issues on Pakistani literature for the *Journal of Commonwealth and Postcolonial Studies* and *Atlanta Review*.

Hold Your Breath
Waqas Khwaja

Ⴓ Onslaught South Asia Series **no 2**

Published in Oxford by The Onslaught Press
11 Ridley Road, OX4 2QJ
1 February 2017

Poems © 2017 **Waqas Khwaja**

This edition © 2017 **Mathew Staunton**

ISBN: **978-1-912111-72-5**

Cover includes a detail from *Der Mönch am Meer* by Caspar David Friedrich

Typeset in Jean Francois Porchez's **Le Monde Livre** and **Le Monde Sans** inside
with Akira Kobayashi's **Din Next** on the cover

Designed & edited by **Mathew Staunton**

Printed & bound by Lightning Source

For Michael Rothenberg
and Terri Carrion
with warmest regards
[signature]
Sept. 18, 2017

Dedicated to the memory of Eric Garner
whose last words "I Can't Breathe"
remain for me
the most potent metaphor
for our age

Contents

I'm Nobody! Who are you?
Are you—Nobody—too?

Emily Dickinson

Coat

It was a place of flying horses
and centaurs dancing
You brushed my cheek with your lips
but never noticed
the shabby coat I wore
only the eye
that dreamed

Like a second skin
I wear my coat
passable outside
but its lining worn
and still it warms me
and still you try to look
past its faded indifferent browns

It is not time
but people
and it is not people
but people in a certain
recital of their lives
whose spirit sings
to the mandolin sun

then taste is sharp
and the nose picks up
all the secret
smells and enticements
and just a tiny
quiver of a hand
sets the skin alight

Here take my coat
and shake it out
and see what tumbles forth
Ah, the centaurs
can you believe it
and flying horses
and there goes the mandolin
bright as ever

Going Back

Not this time—
No, it does not feel like home
All is familiar as before
Nothing seems to have changed
Covered in dust
Leaves hang limp
Birds struggle
To find shade
Faltering, fluttering
Their ragged dry wings
Dogs slink away
Resignedly
Chased all day
By a savage sun
And tar oozes from roads
That sizzle and sputter
Under speeding wheels
While dirty homespun awnings
Are lowered deep
Over roadside stores and stalls
To keep out the fiery air

Not this time—
Though in late afternoons
When shadows seep
Into declining light
Just as they did
Twenty years ago
And perhaps thirty before that
Long lines of children
Women and defeated men
Form at municipal
Hand pumps and hydrants
Each clutching hopefully
A pitcher, a plastic pail, or a jug

Chattering away as they wait
Occasionally breaking
Into exasperated arguments
And all go suddenly quiet
Slumping a bit
When word travels down
That water has
Stopped once more

Nothing seems to have changed
People curse and complain as usual
Make a few lewd remarks
Then rouse themselves
With gossip, jokes, tall tales
Until there is something
At last really to cheer about
One hour of light
After two without it
Water suddenly flowing again
A cool breeze picking up
A surprising tail-end resistance
Before eventual loss
A minor sporting victory
After a string of defeats
Rains unexpectedly
After a month of hellish sun
An unusual judicial challenge
To martial rule
A lone voice
Against a culture of deception

Not this time—
Though nothing seems
To have changed
Generators purr away

In walled mansions
Electric motors pull
All water for private use
While people wait at public hydrants
Honest leaders
Remain dull as ever
The smart make money on speculation
And the military
Gorges itself on privileges
Saving discarded scraps
For pet radicals and politicians
Fussy bureaucrats
Quietly pocket their pickings
Justices cash in
On a timely decision or two
And bankers maintain secrecy
To protect themselves and their clients

Where I live now
The fight is all about fuel
Not water
Billions of gallons are flushed down
With toilet paper every day
And many more
Spiked with lethal
Chemicals and carcinogens
Injected down earth's throat
To access oil and gas
Then discarded
When the job is done
To leach
Into underground water
Sullying its very source
And the pumped waste
Drained into open pits

To evaporate
Into air and cloud
And return man's bounty
With deadly rain

No display of want
Is acceptable
If they must
Folks die behind closed doors
Silently
Soiled in their own filth
Still clutching half-opened cans
Of cat and dog food
Or grub retrieved
From garbage dumps
Mired in disease
Malignant with longing and loneliness
Nameless in neglect
Denied comfort
Or solace
Or alleviation from pain
Homeless and reviled
Huddling under bridges
Or in abandoned lots
Or bundled at the entrance
Of some magnificent shut door

The affluent don't
Offend at all
Especially when no shadow afflicts their skin
Their addictions
A sport
Their groping
Only locker room fun played out in real time
Their fears of colored folk

Legitimate, well-founded
Their filching clever
Their deceptions commendable
They operate without fear
While, the destitute are, well
Destitute in all things
Except the taint of their epidermis
And carefully kept that way
Only ostentatious displays
Of wealth and indulgence are reverenced
And synthetic assets
Especially among
Celebrities and swindlers

But reputations are fracked clean
Of their oil and gas
Just as calmly
With unsparing inevitability
When the bearer is like the earth
Stained with its mineral browns and black
Prison houses teem
With the traffic of a people
Broken early into a realization
Of their home away from home
Sometimes domiciled for life
For a few milligrams of weed
A petty theft or alleged assault
Or more grievously for graver crimes
Indigence and illiteracy
For deprivation and guilt
Are inked into the hide
That covers their bones
And masks their faces
More food is discarded every day
Than can feed an entire continent

Back where I started
Our dividends match
The investments we made
Try praying in a mosque
In a church, a temple, or at home
Alone or in groups
Try visiting a sick friend
A relative in a hospital
Attend a wedding
Or a funeral
Be a good Muslim
Or a bad one
A Christian, Hindu, whatever
Recite Sufi poetry if you will
Pretend you are English
And fairer than the fairest of them
Or the scorned and shunned local
Blending with the crowd
There's a man in headgear
Waiting for you
There are bullets printed
With your name on them
Bombs and shrapnel
That carry your DNA
Wherever you go

Triptych

I

At fifteen I had not yet seen the sea:
driving toward the beach I picked up first
the smell of fish and salt strong in the air,
then particles of sand against my face,
the sea itself, flounced and frilled, crested with
tufts of brushwork foam, dirty white atop
pale green, and blue-black waves, sang with sounds
of far off lands, a subterranean roar
that called and promised much but never quite
revealed its source, soft wet sands subsiding
beneath the foot before they held, then gave
again as wave after rolling wave dashed
against my body, leapt, shattered, and swept
back again, the next one taller, stronger
than before, its whip and splash curling on
itself, sands splitting to reveal mollusks
and shells of fervid colors and shapes, each
a treasure that I eagerly gathered:
flat fan shapes, crowned whorls, and tiny spotted
shells singing with life behind serrated
lips—and creatures of the sea crawled between
my toes and through them tickled their way
across my foot and up my leg, before
another gathering wave crashed and washed
them away, even as I stepped upon
yet another embedded shell and curled
my toes to pick it up and add to my
growing collection—yet, even the next
morning, when I woke up, a strange, putrid
smell filled the room and swirled elusively
around as I looked in closet and drawer,
beneath the bed, and sniffed my shoes and socks
to find its source, till, suddenly, I stopped
short and realized with a sinking heart
it rose from that small treasure bag beside

my bed, oh, from all the bewitching shells
I had gathered the day before, and I
poured out its contents in the bathroom sink
and washed them clean of all decaying worms
and expired life—but ever after
enticed by what till then I had not known
I have yearned for the sea, coast, beach and all,
the hollow boom and crash from distant shores,
the smell of fish, salt particles in the breeze,
the yielding wet slate sand beneath my feet—

II

and hills till I was twelve, when dry heat drove
us north, traveling by train, my first, and all
the way wandering dreamscapes of boyhood years
with an imaginary friend, before
transferring to a bus that dragged itself
groaning over a steep hill road, climbing
higher with each tiered and winding groove
precariously in narrowing rounds right up
the mountain's side—a new perspective
opening up, houses seen on level ground
now far below, nestled in what revealed
itself as valley, the fertile lap, hill
upon hill, mountain peaked by higher mountains,
endlessly offered to habitation,
and a dazzling mercury vein I knew
as streamlet at the bridge an hour ago,
amidst it all, threading its path past field,
forest, and grove, and over pebbled bed—
through tiny street-wide towns and villages
with all their wares spilled out beside the road,
their fruits, and wicker crafts, and nuts, and shawls,
till in the middle of nowhere, the air
already chill, brook water running freely
down the metaled road, we stopped to cool
the engine and drink our fill—beyond this
clouds drifted across streets, and muslin mists
slipped through forests of pine and spruce,
slid around cottages far below, ran
through walnut leaves and sprouting foliage—
another hairpin turn, another stiff climb,
and with a last heave and stammer the bus
arrived, and at that instant tarnished the dream
with diesel fumes and honking cars, the growl
and grumble of buses and trucks, their brakes
squealing, the noise all at once of crying

porters, hotel touts, street venders, beggars,
shoe shines, helpers, the site transformed
to a trading station on an ancient
route—a new kind of magic cast its spell,
a new sorcery of din and chatter—
but in the night when from a cottage window
I glanced below, my heart forgot a moment
how to beat, then came alive suddenly
entranced like a paper kite in the wind—
down in the darkness the valley was aglow
with firefly lights waving their trifling flames,
and a cool breeze from some deep dark hollow
revived with it a dreamscape memory:
a timid absent hand and a promise
of love's first blossoms on the lips.

III

How strange, that none of this compares
with the city I have lost, the city
that first gave me life, whose air I inhaled
with my first breath, where I grew up and went
first to school—the site of my first transgression,
the city where I loved, and lost, and won,
in that order and no order at all,
separately and all together, at the same time—
dearer to me are its streets and lanes, its
dying sacred river, its flat terrain,
where everything once came without seeking,
as mulberry suddenly on spring trees,
its dust more precious than dreams and promises
of glittering lands and seas, mountains and rivers—
dearer to me is the city I have lost,
dearer all friends and foes of my youth,
the years of my early disaffection,
dearest the absent ones—
helpless before the dust of my birth land
whose pores and particles are my pores and cells,
whose undistinguished gray and brown birds,
now on a ledge, now at the window sill,
homely and familiar, now fluttering in the branches
of a thick-leaved pipal, now chirping in a stately sheesham,
all settle to comfort in some city that grows
and pulsates within, in its dusty streets
and cool lanes, in its crowded, noisy places,
on the leafy branches of its trees—
O' ruined city!, except in memory,
except in these inadequate words I write,
the shades and colors of your passing seasons,
the creek that sluiced water from the canal
feeding nurseries of garden plants, flowers, and trees
on its way beyond, to fields
and washing spots on its banks in the suburbs,

the open sewage with its foul, damp smells
running by the walls of gated mansions,
your gardens and parks
a refuge for young and old, for poor and rich alike,
the lighted amaltas, the flowering kikar,
gul mohur, sumbal, gul-e-nishtar,
each breaking into its blossoming red and gold
your fruit trees,
mango and guava, the favorite haunts of parrots,
the transplanted lichi,
bounteous in its foreign soil,
the native jaman fattening in summer rain,
helpless before your abundance
helpless before your contradictions
helpless before your dust
O my city!

Farewell

for Parveen Shakir

The day, after all, has
its own darknesses, the night
its own sleepless shimmers

Where would I be
were I not here? Where indeed
if not among strangers and outsiders
as I am here?

         And so she is gone
her deep-tinted flame
so eager to burn itself out?

         And so she is gone
while part-time scribblers
slap each other's hands
and laugh their commonplace laughter
over worn-out jokes?

Poor day, poor night
and poorer still, I
who cannot laugh or weep
nor share my grief

Who do I shake by the shoulder
and reminisce about her?
Who do I look in the eye and say
She too has left us?

Far from the land of my birth
I live in abjection
knowing it has changed forever

knowing that like her
those whom I hold dear
one by one would take their leave

I stare at the horizon
and see nothing in between
as I begin my count

Five Wives I Am Married To

Five wives I am married to
and carry on with a secret lover
devoted to each equally
to all together and separately
but I have neither guilt nor shame
for this or that, for one or other
nor care for those who would heap blame
like a pail of waste upon my head
curse and damn and wish me dead
some creed, I am told, permits only four
others prescribe monogamy
I care for neither one nor other
nor for a hundred milkmaids who
dance to delight a god or two
my five mates I will have and keep
though share them with all most willingly
my lover too, I do not care
if she warms another's bed
she is free to go and sleep
with whomsoever she chooses to
yet when she comes to me and brings
her musky flanks, her tulip lips
her spiced breath, my spirit sings
my parched bodyscapes long dead
awaken in a thousand tiny nibs
alert to her mouth that blows on them
and all at once erupt in bloom
and there in earth's uncloistered room
sound, taste, and smell, taction, and sight
come together in a dithyramb
of unpremeditated delight

Meander

for Gabriel Rosenstock

The precise description
the exact denomination
the particularized evocation
is not just a trope
not just myth
but the starting point of all mythologies

Generalization effaces
planes out, covers up
what is in fact
intricate, twisted, or coiled
mottled and coarse
fissured and creviced and creased

Intimately what evokes
the personalized special
the startling distinct
initiates it—
the audacious ride
the dipping, soaring, hurtling flight
the aimless meander
into imagination's unsettled
into fancy's inadvertencies

This poetry we write
all art, all science
to crack the opaque
all but a fleeting fleck
a derelict word
floating past
the vitreous gel
to a tangible illusion
it inveigles and misleads
and brings us but
to a caveat
quick and kindling

i dream of my father

it is as if again
i am getting ready to accompany you
to a district far away
to assist you in another murder trial
assembling all that may
be needed for the journey
daylight sweeping in as I hear
your bright voice in another room asking
is it all done
are we ready

and the next night
i am at a table at our old place
making sandwiches and packing slices of teacake
when you enter suddenly
but i
just at that instant, inexplicably
find the sandwiches dwindled
the cake gone entirely
and, embarrassed, look about in confusion

they were for you, yes
though it was you always who prepared
the sandwiches, got the teacake you liked
but where did they vanish
now it would be contemptible to serve
you a poor collation when we stop for tea
and there are only two, perhaps
three, pieces left

both dreams entering soundlessly
my sleep world, one night following another
a month after you passed on—
meaningless probably
passing apparitions
but i can't get them out
of my head

for the days of my apprenticeship with you
come back to me
when all the audacity of my youth
the swagger and feigned conviction
floated on the dazzling slipstream of your renown
while others just smiled and suffered it for your sake

but case files and travel bags are real
the smooth milk-tea colored sleeves for legal briefs
nap of worn paper in my palms
the bookish scent of law digests
their solemn black and brown binding

real too, the smell of fresh-baked bread
the rich chicken paste seasoned with cracked black pepper
the lavishly buttered egg-spread spiced with mustard
flavored with crushed mint leaves, and you

with your deep resonant voice
your signature smoker's smell
not yet plagued by resentments and disagreements

nor by the clogged arteries or the cancer on your tongue
the warm magnitude of your presence

just as real as sunshine on my face

*say no words
time is collapsing
in the woods*

from *14 haiku* by Sonia Sanchez

piya torey nain

(Sketch for Khayal in Raag Sakh)*

beloved your eyes
                          your eyes
            eyes
eyes
            your eyes
                          beloved
beloved your
      your
                  your eyes
              be
                  lov
                        ed
    be
laa aa aa aav
  ed
                      be
laav
                  ed
your eyes
                  your eyes
your aa aa aa aa ees
    pi yaa aaa torey nai aayan

piyatoreynain piyatoreynain piyatoreynain

look this way
turn towards me
show your grace
your regard
for what I suffer

afflicted
I touch your feet
preserve my shame
my credit, my trust

belov ed
       belov ed your
                  belov ed your
    belov ed your eyes
            be
           lov
              ed
                 your eyes
eyes
      aeyes
           aa aa aa eees
                    aaa aaa aaa eees
gamapa gamapa gamapadasa gamapadasa
mapadenada mapadenada denada denada
danedapadhoom dhoomtaderena
danedapadhoom dhoomtaderena
danedatanoom tanoom
danedatanoom
tanaderena tanaderena
tananaderenaan noomtaderenaan
tananaderenaan noomtaderenaan
tannanaderderdeen tana dere naan
tannanaderderdeen tana derey naan
tananaderderdeen tananadereynaan
tananaderderdeen tananadereynaan

*In homage to classical singers
Ustad Amanat Ali Khan and Ustad Fateh Ali Khan*

Primer

N
am
mu
A
nu
Nin
mah
Brah
ma
Brah
man
Rah
man
Bra
ham
Ab
ra
ham
Bra
heem
Ib
ra
heem
Ra
heem
Ab
ram
Ab
ra
ham
Ram
Ra
am
Ra
ma

Ma
ra
Ma
ree
am
Ma
ry
am
Ma
ry
Ye
su
Iss
a
Mas
ih
Yah
weh
Ye
shu
ah
Je
su
Je
sus
Chr
ist
Chr
is
tna
Chr
ish
ma
Kri
sh

na
Ra
dha
Ra
dhay
Ra
am
Rab
Rab
ba
Ab
ba
Ra
am
Si
ta
Sat
Sat
guru
Sat
nam
Ra
am
Li
la
Lil
ith
Al
lat
La
ila
ha
Alo
ha

Ha
Shem
il
Al
lah
Lil
lah
Li
la
Ra
am
Li
la
La
illa
ha
El
o
him
il
Al
lah
Kal
ma
Ka
li
ma
Maa

unclassified i

unclassified i
neither one nor its other
from sea nor sand
river nor land

father, my home
i leave behind
mother, this knot
i now unbind

my days of play
in your backyard over
your threshold strange
like a mountain range

days of laughter
left on a stone
a shadow of vanished
flesh and bone

four carriers adorn
my traveling litter
and bear it upon
shoulders that glitter

my very own
and those unknown
recede slowly
from my lingering eye

man nor woman
beast nor snake
fish nor fowl
real nor fake

father, keep your home
it was not meant for me
i leave now for
a far country

Poetry for Peace

Sounds good, doesn't it
alliteration, assonance, all that stuff
But, come!
Are we indeed
so ready to believe

When was it ever so
Name your poet or prophet
(Is there a difference)
Neither accepts the other
Self-willed, both

Rejects searching for honor
through words baked
in the heart's raging kiln
Lovers of ruins, of crumbling walls
of what is broken and cannot be fixed

Lovers of forests, wastelands
bald crags and boulders
carrying an oasis of palm trees
a secret well of water within
brackish and sweet

Deserts seared with sands
deserts frozen under icy moons
habitats of a heart's
dark alluvium
feeding the stem of their soul

breaking out in unlikely fruit
spiked flowers, scarred clay fragments
shed blood sap
bushes barbed with burning words
radiant mirages over a bleak horizon

Name your prophet or poet
singers and charmers of a day and night
those warblers stretching their necks
pouring forth songs
that scald their throats

spinning round and round in dream and delusion
like a planet in imagined homage
recluses, nobodies
addressing nobodies, everybody
entertainers only, too earnest sometimes

Who should I tell, mother
the travails of separation
A man in appearance
a woman within
I toil through a pathless jungle

Who, once entering
ever left
Who, seeking, found
Harmony and concord indeed
Peace

Hold your breath

Hold your breath
for the day is gone
and half the night
it is already late
and if ever
dawn breaks out, you
my friend will never know

Ah, hold your breath
silence itself will teach
you what you need to know
the day is gone
and half the night
and what is left
it too will pass

If your eyes darken
let your eyelids fall
if your heart bleeds
let it find release
the day is gone
and half the night
tomorrow this desert
may come to bloom
but you will not know

Kughu Kohrray

Doves and horses
dumb birds and beasts
hoopoes and goats
come look, come look

pigeons and cattle
rabbits and lizards
they are all for you
run up and see

Here's a parrot with
a hole in its neck
and if you blow through it
like this, see me do it

it's a whistle as well
blow hard or blow softly
it makes a sweet sound
come try this one out

And so all these others
have no sound of their own
but only what you give them
by blowing through the hole

You give them your breath
you give them your voice
it's almost as if
they stir in your hands

Clay toys, shaped and molded
and baked in a fire
clay doves and clay horses
each one just for you

A cart and its wheels
with axle and spokes
an ox yoked to it
or a pair if you wish

There's more if you like
much more than all this
let me untie this bundle
and show you what else

Look, here, a mud oven
All ready for use
Come close, you can touch it
It won't come apart

Pots, serving trays, and saucers
clay skillets and pans
bowls, sifters, colanders
jars, dishes, and spoons

Here's a pestle, and a mortar
to grind your spices
and all that you can wish for
take your pick, or take it all

You just need a house
you just need a household
and everything to run it
is here for the asking

And when you are done
and tired of it all
you may toss these away
without worry or care

Our mother, this earth
will take them all back
and rains wash and sweep them
down rivers and creeks

Into ponds and pools
into waterholes and bogs
and again I will venture
as I have long done

Forever and a day
through seasons and years
and dredge up the loam
the pitch and the clay

And once again knead it
and mold it and sculpt it
in forms that you see
in shapes that you love

Doves and horses
dumb birds and beasts
hoopoes and goats
I bring them to you

pigeons and cattle
rabbits and lizards
they are all for you
run up and see

Last Spring

1
Is it Arab or Hebraic spring?
Or sputtering dawn of a burning cross?
The cauldron seethes and hisses.
A murky brew rises
and boils over.
Watch it spread.

2
Spring soot
And winter ash
Autumn bile
And summer spite

3
The magpie is blue,
raven, and white; its beak red,
steel grey, or yellow.

4
I am one
of no color
impossible to track.
When I brand my writ on you
you bruise black
you bleed red.

5
The magpie refuses
to be classified. At
times its tail is green, its
head and wings
chestnut, its back and breast
azure of many shades
or pea, olive, or turquoise.

Rose legs, or granite grey. And bill
coral, mustard, or black.
For all that simply
a relative of crow.

6

And crow has a harsh bark
is a sapient bird with a flinty beak.
It ushers no spring
but cares for its kind
shares food with its flock.
It feeds on fruit and grain
on earthworms and crop pests
frogs, lizards, and young mice
minnows and fish
even carrion.
It raids nests for eggs and hatchlings.

7

A shadow of no color hovers over earth's spring
a blazing light that dazzles eyes
and differentiates into a rainbow's bars.
White light vibgyors into leaf and flower
infects bird and beast with tint, pigment, and paint.

8

Crow stays stubbornly black
casts its shadow on spring, summer, autumn, winter.
Crow shades eyes
dark as darkness alone
dark as truest blood.
Crow circles above and warns.
Crow comforts.

9
A murky brew
stirred with exquisite malice
spitting tarnish and taint
hissing slander and calumny
while fiery cloudlets of smoke
rise to entrance
invisible nostrils.
Crow watches attentively.

10
The magpie feeds on caterpillars
flies, beetles, and grasshoppers.
It sups on small rodents and snakes
decaying flesh of animals
and scraps left over by predators.
It too steals eggs and nestlings
from other birds.

11
Hunted and trapped
pursued by assassins and slayers
poisoned by baits
indiscriminate epicures
perceived as a menace
their roosts blown up by dynamite
neither eats its kind.

12
Crow pecks and prods ash
and cinder, stabs at charred flesh.
Magpie eyes and waits.

13
The magpie looks in
a mirror and sees many
birds, many colors.

Crow looks at magpie
its eye glittering, and caa-caas
in acknowledgement.

Deep jis ka mehalaat maen he jalay
Chand logon ki khushion ko lae kar challay
Who jo saaey maen har maslehat kip allay
> *Aisay dastoor ko, subhay baenoor ko*
> *Maen nahin maanta, maen nahin maanta*

> 'Dastoor'

A code whose flame shines only in palaces
Guides only a few on the road to happiness
That prospers in the shadow of every expedience
> *Such a code of life, such a dawn without light*
> *I do not recognize, I do not accept*

> 'Code', Habib Jalib

I would have liked to tell you
The story . . .
> *Had they not slit my lips.*

> 'Slit Lips', Samih al-Qasim

I was born an enemy

I was born an enemy, but I did not know it then
The Sandman came and shut my eyes
The Clatterer lurked in dark corners waiting to pounce
And only a sacred verse kept it at bay
In the morning I was the sparrow and its mate
In the afternoon a dog looking for shade
Come evening, a woman whose glimpsed hair flashed in the sun's
    dying light
As she flung it back bathing in a stall without a roof
At night a mouse pretending to be a lion's companion
Sometimes a prince dispossessed of his state

I was born in many lands
I have traveled across many seas
Scaled mountains and trekked through timeless deserts
I have been many people
Mujhay dekho tau sahih meray jism kay kitnay tukrray hain
Ek ek hissa kabhi jis ka naam tha
Aur wo apnay naam sey pahchana jata tha
Aaj gumnaam hae

Yes, each part of my body had a name once
Cherished and pleasing
No more
Like me, it is now without a name
Kuchh nahin, kuchh bhi nahin
A nameless fragment of many wholes
And those wholes with no face, no hands, arms, eyes, ears, legs, feet
Those wholes without a heart, lungs, liver, guts
Those wholes that have but one designation now, a generic one
Dushman
I was born an enemy, but I did not know it then

I read about myself in books growing up
Not knowing yet of race or color, caste, class, or creed

Not understanding yet differences in belief
Oblivious to gender
And I affianced myself with those who taught me,
With the language they spoke,
And those who wrote the books I read,
Their ideas and their judgments
And I came to see myself as a stranger in my own land
As an alien among those I grew up and lived with
As one unfamiliar with a language my own
But a confrere of those that brought to me the flames of their scripted
    words

And I learned one by one all shades of difference
I learned race and color, caste, class, and creed
I learned beliefs
Calibrated carefully to context
Those that must be despised and those held in esteem
I learned to separate myth from religion
Religion from legend, parable, and fable
I learned some tales were history, some history legend
That what was outside the province of a preceptor's intimacy
Was all fable and superstition
A false shadow of the real and the true

I learned gender, male versus the female
Biologically and mentally at odds with each other
Each behaving in ways ascribed to each to maintain integrity of kind
One above the other, always
But differently in different societies
Oppressive and abusive in mine
Broadly coordinate and honored (within a play of delicate differentials)
In another I learned to deduce inclinations and attributes from the
    penis and the vulva
And the relationship of one to other of tiller and tilth
In my world exploitative, in another cultured and cultivated

No matter how intensely I learned to admire those who taught me
Strove to observe laws and etiquette they had established
Honor their rules, precepts, and axioms
Respect and celebrate even their rituals of euphemism and equivocation
Their subtleties of differentiation
I was not the right color, the right race
Not from the right society, not the right society
That I aspired fruitlessly, and entirely at my own risk, for things
    unattainable
That I was born an enemy, and my learning but to establish
The unalterable nature of this simple truth

Caliban to those who taught me, forever a suspect
Waiting for a chance to rape some underage Miranda
Waiting to overthrow some sage and learned Prospero
Forever conspiring, forever prone to treachery
Forever preparing to commit an atrocity
Polluting with my foul thoughts and native words the language of my
    masters
Born to the wrong people, with the wrong genealogy
In the wrong place, with wrong beliefs
The wrong color, the wrong aspirations
I was born an enemy, though I did not know it

And here I am, a peevish and fretful poet
Clumsy and uneasy as I recover
Almost as if by accident
Bits and pieces of lost, severed, and discarded selves
Torn limbs and body parts that once were mine
From the maqtal, the wael-feld, that is my present
From the wasteland that is also the graveyard of histories
Primitive and odd, contemporary and outdated
Neither this nor that in the wilderness of life
Adrift in vagaries of gendered forms
Beyond race in the power play of races

Of no class, or status, or rank
Woh jis ki koi auqaat nahin, koi wuqqat nahin
Fighting, I am told, modernity and progress
With a combustible mix of words and worlds
Cross-pollinated by strangered languages
Stoked by a kindling of wild thoughts
Dukhan di roti, soolan da salan, ahaan da balan
Caught between damning desire and deadly rage
Forever condemned to render my dry bones
As the final offering at the altar of indifference

Yet why does my heart falter when I look up and find
You, armed and ready among those I am preparing to resist?

I am afraid of Muslims

I am afraid of Muslims
Christians unnerve and alarm me
Jews fill me with dread
I fear Hindus
I am terrified of Gautama's followers
Scared of Nanak's devotees
Science and art
Secularism and socialism
Capitalism, communism, commerce, civilization
Rattle and dismay me

An ominous firelight flares up in my brain
The moment I see a human figure
And I flee in terror
To deserts, forests, and hills
To rivers, lakes, and seas
To haunts of birds and beasts
The domains of fish and eels
Of sharks, dolphins, and whales
To worlds of insects and worms, of all burrowing creatures
To realms of reptiles, serpents, and snakes

Contiguous worlds
Without rituals of aversion
Without philosophy, religion, law
Without affliction of private visions
Where no species inflicts its language on another
No species its lexicon, its call, its order, its practice
Where life itself is art, living, science
Contiguous worlds
Of simple sorrows, simple joys
Without raptures and ecstasies
Without gnawing of the vitals in envy and spite
Where pain does not devolve to depths of despair
Nor killing bloom into calamity no words may adequately contain

Contiguous worlds
Now turned into garbage bins, into litter pits
Into radioactive disposal dumps
In collective indifference
Contiguous worlds
To which malign effluents leach and spread irredeemably
Where plants of infections and defilement pitch their roots
    deep into the earth's core
Contiguous worlds
Invaded and annexed
Ruptured, and torn, and robbed

Look, look, I cry out
The stockpiles they have assembled
The toxic malice of their words and deeds
The malevolence of their contempt
The impunity of their depredations
The freedom of their slaughter
Oblivious to what is seeded
Oblivious to what they foment
Unmindful of ruin and havoc
Blind to the obliteration
They have prepared for themselves

But the plains smile and shake their heads
Deserts stretch out on their backs and snigger
Mountains, caverns, and rocks ring with laughter
And waters of the earth dissolve in wild guffaws

Today I am a Muslim weaver

Today I am a Muslim weaver in love with a Brahmin
boy And we will be one through all the years of our life
In death, we will be buried side by side
Though we will die some years apart
I take leave of the mosque and the madrassa
But you will celebrate yearly my soul's union in my demise
And when you do, you will celebrate him with me
My name begins with his name
When you remember him, his name will always precede mine

Now I am the son of Mu'mina Khatoon
Learning my alphabets at my father's knee in a mosque
Seeking wisdom in the forest of scriptures and jurists' words far and wide
But tonight I meet the mendicant from Tabriz
And we fall into each other's arms body and soul
I do not know yet that I will lose him in four years
I do not know yet that he will inhabit me for the rest of my life on earth
That he writes all I will write
But I do know my tomb is in the hearts of those who remember me
    always with him

Another day, and I am a supplicant traveling from Kasur to Lahore
My ancestry is impeccable, but I travel on foot, lowest among the lowly
The shimmer and dazzle of sacred verses boxed in my heart
But I seek a guide worthy of what I carry in secret within
And here is one turning the soil, hoeing around plants, Weeding,
    watering his garden
There is nothing to it, he says
What's uprooted here is planted elsewhere
I shed my man's clothing and put on a whore's outfit and bells
And dance for him in the streets to win his heart

Oh, and a throng of devotees fawns upon me today
Gathered around my rope-bed (Guardian of Saints, they call me, my
    pupils and my disciples)
But waiting for him my eyes have become the skylight of my room

I know he will come triumphant from his expedition months after I
    am gone
He with whom I danced one spring in fields of endless sarsoon
And he will know the moment he steps into the courtyard
I see him weeping and wasting away at my feet mumbling the words
    he will compose
My sweetheart sleeps on her wedding bed, her hair covering her face
Go to your home Khusrau, night falls in the darkened realm

And I am today a black, lesbian, feminist, mother, poet warrior
Close to my death, I know, because of my malignant breast
I have loved women and men equally, or almost equally
White or black hardly mattered to me, but my own blackness does
For I claim that as much as I claim my sex, my womanhood
And at this stage, nearing my death I think of how I smelled that day
When my mother, her hands dried after her washing
Looks at me lying on the couch, and she comes to me
And without a word we touch and caress our most secret places

Suddenly, I am in Lesbos surrounded by friends and companions
Aware we are more deeply bound to each other than to our husbands
Though our husbands have their place too
Go, and be happy, but remember (you know well) who you leave
    shackled by love
But to give and receive love beyond mere lovemaking
To strike the lyre and dance to song and music
Pour myrrh upon each other's head, bathe in the pools together
Kiss and rub each other dry, there is much the world counts beautiful
I say, indeed, it is whatever you desire

I am the woman who leaves her husband to go her own way
For I will not lie under him who was created simultaneously with me
Nor endure his subjection
Nor the insults or abuse by in-laws
You may find me naked roaming the streets without shame

You may find me in bed with other women who are my sisters and
    my lovers
You may find me alone braving the forests and the wilderness
I will choose for myself whatever it is I wish to do
I am the first rebel, the first to be exiled for my beliefs

And it is I who say to my mother-in-law after my husband dies
Do not press me to leave you or to turn back from following you!
Where you go, I will go. Where you lodge, I will lodge.
Your people shall be my people, and your God my God.
Where you die, I will die, and there will I be buried.
And for her I will bear a child by another man
To be her comfort and her redeemer
And faintly I see in the distance, in some hazy desert morning
What seems like a man slowly bleeding to death outstretched on an
    upright cross

And body to body, lip to lip, our arms encircling each other
Today I know neither sex nor color, creed nor rank
Black entwined with white, brown with pale
No garment but our bodies, no raiment but our desire
Our tongues seeking each other's mouth, our breasts to breasts conjoined
Androgynous both, both complete, not partly this or partly that
Created together in that cosmic cauldron
I am one, I am many, I am all of you, my tale has never been told
I am just trying to tell the story

Look at my face. See how you have disfigured me.
I don't know myself from myself anymore.
What do I do if I have no urge to make love to a woman,
Or to a man when I am a woman
And you compel me to marry one? Or if I love as I choose? or if I do
    not wish to make love at all?
What do I do if I end up living as a shade in shadows? As a ghost among
    real people?

If my life becomes one enormous lie, and I do not wish to live a lie?
What if that cankers me from within, and someone, someone I love, is
   oblivious to it?
Look at me. I have nowhere to go. No one I can trust. Not myself. Not
   even you.
Who do I owe allegiance? Why don't you recognize me?

Yes. They Were My Eyes.

Yes. They were my eyes. But first it was
the tongue that bothered them. They removed
the larynx and this at least took care of all that
uncontrolled, ungoverned talk they heard that so
annoyed them. But this was not enough either.
The tongue still wagged, even if its words were
not very clear, and they thought this was all

triggered by what the eyes saw, or could see
if allowed to have their way. So that's when keeping
them wide-open, they drilled through the cornea,
and when even that did not quite allay their anxiety,
they had to find other means to prevent what wasn't
supposed to be seen even as a clouded image.
So they scooped them out and preserved them

in a bottle they then gave me to carry home
with me, as a reminder of how the indiscretion
of seeing too much could only result in incapacitation
and removal of that organ of vision. But I could hear
still, and smell, and that came to plague them
with new fears, for hearing what was not authorized
to be heard, and smelling events and incidents

when to a normal nose no such odor was detectable,
was clearly a sign of some disorder, an alarming
derangement of the senses that needed to be fixed.
Thus they removed the olfactory receptors, to begin with,
and with one stroke, they also killed the sense of taste—
before they turned their attention to the faculty
of hearing. Some joker suggested that while

I was in their power, they might as well
cut off my ears. That done, they pierced through
the tympanic membrane, through the ossicles

in the middle ear, right into the cochlea, and drained
it of all its fluid. Then they let me go, but my feet
were unsteady, and I could barely walk, so this
time they did not provide a jar with pickled water

to carry with me the ears they had lopped off. It
seemed, however, that the wagging tongue, though it
had difficulty making words, still troubled them. A day
later I was called back, and just as a matter of preemptive
caution, that tongue was sliced off. Take that, they
said. You should be safe now, from yourself and us!
Now all I have left is touch—this body, and what

it feels on its skin. And touch glows and flowers
in the dark. Touch my cheek, and see how it burns
and softens. Pass your hand over my chest, and
suddenly under your palm it responds, the nipples
stiffen, the flat stomach twitches, and the hair . . .
oh, but hair vanishes under the palps of your fingers
and the hollow of your palm, and before you know it

the chest swells and grows breasts, soft and firm
at the same time, urgent for recognition. You move
down the body, the hips, lean at first and slim,
begin to round out and ease a bit, pliant and elastic . . .
in the middle, the penis, like a piece cut from a stem
of sugarcane in a clump, recedes and retreats
under your fingers, becomes a clitoris, nestled

in the sanctuary of the vagina, and down, down
further, the muscled thighs and shanks turn
and transform smooth and sleek under your touch
and the feet are the feet now, fleshy though strong,
that they never were—a wondrous transfiguration,
a metamorphosis like never seen before but at
the beginning, the very beginning of all things.

They would have liked to kill me. But who
would clean their bathrooms and their kitchens?
Who would till the soil, and plant, and harvest
the crops for them? Who would nurture the orchards
with their sweat, and pick out the best of fruits
for them? And who would do all their menial work?
Bring up and teach their children? Fight their battles for them?

Sans eyes, sans ears, sans tongue, bereft of the sense
of smell, I am all body, I am all touch, I am all feeling.
And even this scares them. They would have to kill me
entirely for me to stop articulating myself through touch,
or disable my brain completely for the body to not
transmit its signals of pleasure, and joy, and protest.
But what use would I be, then, for them?

Words flow out of my hands now.
Words pour out of my fingertips.
Touch becomes feeling becomes thought becomes tongue.
They try to pass laws to forbid feeling.
Touch frightens them now. They wish to forbid touch.
The body frightens them. They wish bodies wouldn't join, wouldn't
    bind, wouldn't interfuse.
But they are helpless now. The body finds its language. The body
    expresses itself.

Tea Party

A lot of tea was tossed on fish that day!
They would have come in pumps and heels and hats,
If only they were asked or had a say!

But no one had a thought for them that day—
The rebels railed against the Townshend Acts
And just flung crates of tea in Boston Bay.

Fish grumbled, indeed, this wasn't quite the way,
Darting away from staining tea-leaf tracts.
If only they were asked or had a say!

Above, roused comrades rushed without delay
To teach a lesson to Westminster rats,
Tossed yet more tea on fish in Boston Bay.

Caught by surprise, fish stared in dismay
As rioters strained to profit plutocrats—
If only they were asked or had a say!

So without a tea- or milk-pot, or a tray,
Without scones, crumpets, biscuits, butter pats,
A lot of tea was dumped on fish that day!
If only they were asked or had a say.

Not for the fainthearted

This is not a poem for the fainthearted
This is not a poem for delicate sensibilities
You may recognize a bit of your world in it

And then . . . but first, this: it is not about
Your fussy pet peeves or personal wellbeing
This is not about how to fulfill your ambitions

Or your disregard for who or what you trample
Underfoot to achieve them; this is not about
Your investments, your dealings on the stock exchange

Have no worry about that, not your offshore
Accounts or shell companies and subsidiary
Corporations, none of that concerns this poem

It does not deal with your bewildering discussions
About interest reduction or interest hikes
Or whether there is a likelihood of inflation or not

Whether enough jobs are being created each month
Or too many people dropping out of the market
Those financial discussions are not its domain

This is not a poem about who deserves subsidies
Which banking and insurance interests are too big
To fail, or about the wisdom of keeping ordinary folk

Reeling under the weight of debt, persuading each
Member of a household out into the marketplace
Or about punishing petty payment lapses and defaults

It doesn't matter to it that this goes on while aiding
Big businesses and rewarding their misconduct and fraud
This poem isn't about that, nor about the rich and famous

Or about the poor and nameless, for that matter, they too
Are not its subject, nor the old, the infirm, the friendless
Folks who cannot take care of themselves nor have

Another to look after them, those without
Healthcare, without food, without shelter, those
With broken homes and hurting parents, without

Schools to educate them, teachers to care
Neglected children of neglected parents
And neglected grandparents, spurned and maligned

None of those, nor the immigrants that flock to this place
With hopes and dreams, or the citizens who wallow
In the stew of their biases and bigotry, the junkies who have no choice

Or those who take drugs as sport and entertainment
Those who peddle and deal in narcotics
Those who are sex workers, or pimps, or traffickers

Of want and youth and vulnerability
Those condemned to a life of misery and abuse
Those condemned only to serve others always

Those for whom the laws have specially been framed
Whether to benefit them or to keep them forever
In servitude, to criminalize them, rob them of all

Vestige of self-respect, of selfhood, those
Whom public safety and justice always
Perceive with alarm and suspicion, or those

Whose special interests make them exceptional indeed
For they can promote or preempt legislation
By putting their acquisitions to good use

This poem is not about them; not about people of
Color either, or what they must suffer or not
Or the first peoples, nor about for-profit prison houses

Women too, and what they must endure in a world
Shaped and governed by men, don't concern
This poem, or whether or not they have rights

Over their bodies or wombs, all this and a lot
More that may be political, economic, or sociological
Is out, out completely, as is war, whatever its cause

And however destructive to human life and nature it is
And whether it is fought conventionally or with drones
With ideas or with chemical weapons, tactical

Or strategic nuclear devices, or merely with economic
Sanctions; so also the idea of justice, or fair play; nor does
Injustice bother it in the least, for this is a poem

Not a political tract, though you may, I grant
Detect a bit of your doing in it, and that might
Just might, create a precarious situation

For you see, though no detonations lie buried
Under its lines, no mines are laid out to trap
You in meaning and connotation, reading it

A certain way, when you recognize a small
Part of yourself in it, may bring about an alignment
Of syllables, words, and syntax you cannot escape

Or if you can, you do not know how—that one
Punctuation mark or syllable that may lead you
To safety or disrupt the process, escapes you

And it starts a searing fuse that singes
A crazy line across your palms, and as you look
At them in disbelief, it explodes in your face

Poof! That, and nothing else. So don't read it
When people you love are around you, and don't
Read it out aloud to anyone. Be careful how you tread its lines.

I told you, this is not a poem for the fainthearted.
This is your world. You created it. This is your poem.
You wrote it out. You read it. You detonated it!

oho ee aggon lang gaya
jais dhayanaen paee

'Maen'

He went by, unnoticed
whose thoughts engulfed me.

'I', Nasreen Anjum Bhatti

We are old men

Your hand casually tapping my arm
Slapping my thigh
I will ignore it
A quiver in the bow of your lip
Your black eyes, frank and forthright
I will perceive and not notice
Later, another will say
"You came to see him today"

We are old men
Wrapped in our Siberias of loneliness
Clouded by fading memories
Entering suddenly the glare of well-lit rooms
Deafened by melodies of young voices

And it is my vanity that surfaces
All over again
I realize in despair

There are books to be read
Songs to be discovered never heard before
Unfamiliar composers, unknown singers
Movies never watched

You educate me all over again
About traversing boundaries
About defying custom and habit
Flouting rules without compunction
Putting me in touch with someone
I left behind a long while ago

It is but a game of pretend and make-believe
You have a gift to make it all seem real
But you scratch at a skeleton in skin here
And your heart will soon be restless again

Even as you seek to breathe into this frame of bones
A passing fancy that it is whole
That blood still courses through it

But it is madness of old age to believe it so
It is madness to believe again

It will all be left behind
Once life recollects itself
From the dream
Here it is but
A last rush of sap
A tremor of spring in sprig and leaf
Before exhausted branches brittle
The tree succumbs to rot
And falls

Yet, in my mind
Just for a fleeting moment
I stretch my hand to seize your arm
And clasp you to myself
As intensely as a hot full moon
Glories in his lordship for a night
Forgetting its borrowed effulgence
From a young summer sun
Whose fool he remains
Through all his phases
Of increase and diminution

While a centipede sits on my face
And slowly eats into the flesh
That remains

Keepsake

Afterwards, if you remember me
Think of me kindly as one who wished
To lose himself in his love entirely
So no self remained but hers whom he loved
Her thoughts, her emotions, her feelings
Her memories, how she thrilled growing up
How she shivered with delight and trepidation
When she first stepped on wet earth
Or the trembling exhilaration when she tasted
Her first orange, or touched another hand
And sensed a light streak through
Straight to her heart, or listened to notes
That awakened within her an ensemble
Of harmonies, or when she first saw
A butterfly slip out of her chrysalis
Or when touch became fragrance, motia
Flowers unfolding, taste on tongue like hearing
Sitar strings plucked in ancient ragas, sight
A melodic rune already melting in her ear
And her being responding with her body
Wholly, intensely, without reserve or
Doubt, before what came in its tow, sadness
And separation, clogging her heart's
Unfettered flow . . . all this and more I came
To feel in a self that was no longer mine
But hers whom I loved, the best part of me
And this is what I've left of mine with you

Variations on a life in dreams

I am obliged
to live a dream I
should not be dreaming

I am in a dream
I could not
even be dreaming

I am striving to live
a dream
I may not be dreaming

I am living
in a dream
I should never be dreaming

I am condemned
to a dream
not of my own dreaming

I am compelled
to live another's dream
that I am dreaming

I am living in
many dreams
I could not be dreaming

There is no escape

You discourse upon violence and aggression
Hypothesize about hurt and torture and harm
About physical abuse, agony, injury
You speculate on deriving pleasure
From inflicting suffering and humiliation
You legitimate and license gratification
From degrading and debasing another
Pushing a body's endurance to see
How much torment it can take
Distress and affliction and disgrace it can suffer
Explore new limits of pleasure
By breaking past frontiers of pain
Overcome revulsion and loathing
Of thought or action, body or site or location
Conquer the brain's flinching
The shudder and recoil of touch
Overcome disgust
Of putrescence, fetid odors, foul smells
In search of experiences that stimulate once more
Step beyond thresholds of control and bondage
Evolving a new aesthetics of servitude and submission
Reach beyond utmost limits of what is possible
So no margins, no boundaries remain
To restrict, or curb, or restrain—

I live through it every day of my life
Not as an abstraction
Or with godlike license and indifference
Not as indulgence
But as a condition of my abasement
Enacted and decreed into my life
I live the effects of it
Its experience in my body's ruin and disfigurement
It is not pleasant
There is no joy in it

No comfort, no rest, no peace
It is rotten through and through
This living out of a life
Even without guilt or remorse
For only if there were no laws to break
Would there be no transgression
Though they come, they come
Don't be mistaken
And bring with them
A sense of inherited worthlessness
An innate culpability

Or, if they don't
The colossal weight of futility
The meaninglessness of all this
The indifference at the heart of
These evolving separated worlds
Of an unraveling multiverse
So maddening in its reticence
So irresistible in its self-display
So impossible to contain
Without creation incessantly of new space
So complete and self-fulfilled
In the smallest particle
So pointless and unnecessary
But for its beauty
But for the beauty it makes possible

what could be stranger

what could be stranger than the way
i experience you?
i taste you with my eyes
smell you with my touch
hear the pores of your skin
humming with bees
see the prickle of your body's
untarnished desire
breathe its stinging melody on my breath
and i sip the ardent voice
of your eyes with my tongue

torn apart

you from me
I from you
we seek our
separate selves

if ever I were
to lose myself
it would only be
in you

if ever you were
to lose yourself
it would perhaps
be in me

lips to mouth
mouth to lips
forever seeking
forever sought

fruitlessly repeating
our broken selves
until somehow
somewhere we

are swallowed up
again
indefinitely by
that infinite chasm

that first gave us
birth as one, then
saw us differentiate
interminably

a word a sigh a voice a light and
i
alone
in a room

'testament', Lucille Clifton

A Simple Poem

This is a simple poem.
It will do nothing for you.
You will read it, and it will be over.
No matter how many times you repeat the experience,
You will not be able to escape the consequence.
Every time you will start to read
It will immediately, already, be done.
Every time you go back to the beginning
And read it all the way through,
You will reach the same result.
And that will be all.
It will be over.
Again and again the same.
But you won't be able to get over it.
You will begin once more, now that you are at the end.
You can try other ways.
Start in the middle,
Anywhere else,
You still will get to the same end.
And, again, that would be it.
Start just anywhere.
In the middle of the line.
Read backwards.
Pick it up at the fourth line from the last.
Or the third from the start, or the end.
Start with the seventh, if you please.
Read it diagonally.
Vertically.
Horizontally.
It will end the same.
Go crisscross over the text.
Read it in any shape you like,
Any pattern you can think of,
Randomly, if you will.
Still the same.

You will start, and it will end.
You will read it, and it will be over.
Try writing it out.
Still the same.
It will do nothing for you.
This is a simple poem.

X

At last, nothing
And exploration of nothing
Shot jouissance
Set on a flat surface
Its colors fading
Its movement played out

I live in the land of the Cyclopes

I live in the land of the Cyclopes
seeking to help them see
with the eye they do not have.
I fear I am losing my vision
in one of my own eyes.

a breath, a word

for Eric Garner

one word
to share with you

one breath
between us

one word
i could not utter

one breath
stuck in my throat

my body's grime
is all my wealth

you excavate me
to find yours

i was a child
without a childhood

a young man
without his youth

my gentleness denied
taught me to love

and love taught me
to invent a life

but my body's grime
could not be washed

my body's grime
would not let me live

ek saans hae
ek lafz
aap kay saath baantnay kay liyay

i can't breathe
i can't breathe

ek lafz jo keh na saka

i can't breathe
i can't breathe

ek saans jo lay na saka

i can't breathe
i can't breathe

meray jism ki mael
he mera kul asasa hae

i can't breathe
i can't breathe

aap meray jism ki kaan ko khod kar
apnain asasay banatay haen

i can't breathe
i can't breathe

ek saans hae
ek lafz
aap kay saath baantnay kay liyay

i can't breathe
i can't breathe

Acknowledgements

A warm thank you to editors of the journals where the listed poems made their earlier appearance, though often in a different form, 'Coat', *Wild River Review* 2012; *Alhambra Poetry Calendar* 2013, *365 Classic and Contemporary Poems*; 'Going Back', *South Asian Review*, Vol. 31, no 3, 2011; 'Triptych', *Vallum, Society for Arts and Letters Education*, 9:1, Winter 2012; 'Farewell', and 'i dream of my father', *Sugar Mule: A Literature Magazine*, Issue 43, 2013; 'Five Wives I Am Married To', 'Kughu Khorray', and 'piya torey naen', *Chicago Quarterly Review*, Winter 2016; 'Primer', *Atlanta Review*, Vol. XX, no 2, Spring/Summer 2014; 'unclassified i', *The Missing Slate*, Issue 9, July 2013; 'I was born an enemy', and 'I am afraid of Muslims', *Poiein Kai Prattein* (poieinkaiprattein.org/poetry); 'I am afraid of Muslims', (with translation in Italian), *Margutte*; and earlier versions of 'Coat' and 'Farewell', published as 'Once' and 'Last Rites', respectively, in original English and in Lithuanian translation, *Poetinis Druskininkų ruduo* 2012.

The epigraphs that mark the beginning of various sections of this collection are drawn from sources which are noted and acknowledged here: Emily Dickinson from *The Poems of Emily Dickinson*, The Belknap Press of Harvard University Press, 1998; Sonia Sanchez from *Morning Haiku*, Beacon Press, 2010; Samih al-Qasim from *Victims of a Map: A Bilingual Anthology of Arabic Poetry*, Saqi Books, London, 1984/2005; Habib Jalib, *Quliyaat e Habib Jalib*, Mavra Books, Lahore, 2007; Lucille Clifton from *The Collected Poems of Lucille Clifton*, 1965-2010, BOA Editions Ltd. Rochester, NY, 2012. Translations of excerpts from the poetry of Habib Jalib and Nasreen Anjum Bhatti are by the author.

Grateful appreciation for friends and friendships that have sustained, inspired, and helped me keep faith in myself and my work: Gabriel Rosenstock, without whose belief and support this book would not have been possible, Michael Rothenberg and Terri Carrion, for introducing me to their remarkable 100 Thousand Poets for Change movement and providing me the opportunity to try my hand at spoken word poetry, Dan Veach, for his quiet encouragement, discerning comments, and useful recommendations that kept me wedded to the art and craft that

goes into the work, Ramsha Ashraf, for her perceptive reading and helpful comments and suggestions, Peggy Thompson, for her unstinting support and conviction, Alan Grostephan, for his generosity in reading through a late draft of the manuscript and offering valuable feedback, and Ilona Yusuf, Hatto Fischer, Ilona Kimberly Nagy, Joy Stocke, Amritjit Singh, Syed Afzal Haider, Moazzam Sheikh, Dr. Nasim Riaz Butt, Furrukh Khan, Franklin Abbot, Rupert Fike, Young Hughley, Laura Shovan, Supriya Kaur Dhaliwal, Youssef Aloui, El Habib Louai, Kerry Shawn Keys, Rafey Habib, Amjad Islam Amjad, Janice Phelps Williams, Moumin Qazi, Mohammad Athar Tahir, Mahboob Ali, Mehboob Ahmad, Irfan Aslam, Mushtaq Soofi, Zia Hasan, Mitali Wong, Martha Woodson Rees, Rosemary Lévy, Zumwalt, Isaac Jack Lévy, and my wonderful colleagues from the English department at Agnes Scott College, Steve Guthrie, Christine Cozzens, Jim Diedrick, Willie Tolliver, Charlotte Artese, Nicole and Jamie Stamant, Robert Myers all, more generally, for the many ways in which they motivated me and the creative spirit that moves me. I am indebted also to the many other well wishers and friends that are not named here but who have always been there for me selflessly with all the abundant generosity and graciousness that defines and describes them.

Special thanks to Dan Veach, Abhay K., Youssef Aloui, Franklin Abbott, Kerry Keys, Dileep Jhaveri, Rati Saxena, Yiorgos Chouliaras, M. A. Niazi, Gabriel Rosenstock, Rafiq Kathwari & K. Satchidanandan for generously finding time to read the manuscript and providing endorsements for this collection.

To Fatima, Omer, Maham, and Murtaza for their love and trust, their excitement about this work, and to Maryam, who has managed me, with my difficult ways and odd hours of work and leisure, and the household these last 38 years of our life together with rare grace and diligence.

other Onslaught poetry titles:

CPSIA information can be obtained
at www.ICGtesting.com
Printed in the USA
FSOW02n0429030717
35716FS